DESIRE

/

HALVES

DESIRE

HALVES

JAI HAMID BASHIR

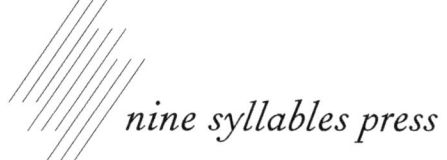

Copyright © 2024 Jai Hamid Bashir
Published by Nine Syllables Press, Northampton MA 01060
First printing, 2024

All rights reserved.
No portion of this book may be reproduced in any form without written permission of the publisher, except by a reviewer, who may quote brief passages in connection with a review for a magazine or newspaper.
Manufactured in the United States of America.
Nine Syllables Press is a proud member of CLMP, the Community of Literary Magazines & Presses.

ISBN 979-8-9881649-1-3

Cover and interior design by Margaret W. Valle
Cover art: Images sourced from Pixabay.

For the Beloved

CONTENTS

Stringing the Bow | 1
Marrow of Mercy | 2
The Strangers | 4
Still, Life with Fruit | 5
On Hunger | 6
The Waiters | 7
Alone, in Halves | 8
Divinities | 9
And the Word for Moonlight is My Name | 10
On Borrowing Noam Chomsky | 13
Aleph from What was Once a Homeland | 14
Madonna Arms | 16
One Red Thread | 17
In Dead Horse Point, We Are Alone, | 18
How to Make an Ariel | 20
Con la Serpiente | 22
Towards Tenderness, A Knife | 23
The Flood | 25
In the Throats of Wild Things | 26
Haptics of Blue | 28
Con La Serpiente Pt. II | 29
Pegasus Tattoo on the Left | 30
Brief Conversation with a Little Moon | 31
The Passenger | 32
The Neighbors | 33
Acknowledgements | 35

World is undivided, observer and observed, as particle from its wave nature,
as prayer from compassionate outcome, when prayer is multiplied
                -Mei-Mei Berssenbrugge

I was driven toward desire by desire
believing that fulfillment of that desire was an end
there was no end
                -Marie Howe

Stringing the Bow

Driving in the American West, reading Celan
and *The Mahabarata*. After the war,
Arjuna drops the bow forged by Brahma back
into the ocean, relinquishing it
back to the gods. Before drowning
in the Seine, Paul Celan wrote that the beloved
is an "arrowy one." Brahmic time is cyclic
and malleable. A blue dress billowing
against an indigo sky. Colorblind
and arthritic, the pregnant heifer milked before
searching for her twins, before being
hit by the Bronco. This time, no one
lives next to the slaughterhouse. The smoldered barn
still stands. The echo of the escaped two-headed
calf rotates around a truck that hasn't had a passenger in
decades. Someone in the farming town remarked, *It looked
like a Hindu god!* Time and love's arrows
inevitability veer from each nock. A hole in the heart,
not for a leak, but a window to let in more light
and the warm storm. *Where are you
going?* I drive on the highway, past
bored animals: how much of our mortality
is an accident? The beloved is a sharpness.
The beloved has an arc. I underline that *time creates and
destroys all things* at the gas station
in my copy of *The Mahabharata*. In a parallel universe, Celan,
shoes filled with water, is drawn onto the bridge, his heart
resuscitated. Verse after verse, I've prayed
in round and rearview mirrors. Blessed with multiple
faces. I take a turn off course. I am so afraid
of ends.

Marrow of Mercy

Releasing the half-eaten olive from my lips,
to create a goat's eye in the center
of my plate as the evening chews

an assemblage of darkness. I kite
my hands over flames as if I control
the underworld as a banquet

or pestilence. Eating is an obedience
to this one body. I only exist
second-hand. People's hands

have been through each sleeve
before me. In a Gabriel García Márquez
story, two lovers don't touch, only meet

in dreams. Then, repeat a solemn refrain:
ojos de perro azul. Last night, I dreamt
of my old beloveds. I begged them

to stay and repeat: *eyes of a blue goat*
in Urdu. یلی بکری کی آنکھ. Etched delicate,
the animal's snowy belly looked

like a slice of winter pear. The hoof,
god-cobbled black, stamped the ground.
It left tallies. It knew choreography.

Everything is more beautiful in Urdu
and Spanish. I have a book report:
I looked for the lovers. I looked far

into canine's pupils, and no dog
I know is blue; they all seemed happy.
My sky-eyed husky killed everything

that trespassed into our dark field. We found
the black-gloved paws of squirrels.
Only thieves in the animal kingdom

have hands like ours. Raccoons, possums,
and hungry monkeys swarmed my halo-
blonde friend touristing India. She messages:

I understand why you worship them. I remind her
I'm Muslim. My old dog slept outside, but we loved
him more than ourselves. I only like dogs

and dogs in this life. When I walk down
the street, I hate making eye contact. Instead, I pray
to *Allah* for mercy for every earthworm.

Ultimately, I want to be eaten
with gentleness in my departure, as I was
nurtured upon arrival. When I was young, Ma

cooked mutton. Despite its braying, I tied
a pretty ribbon, a token of tender despair,
around its neck the evening before goat-Eid.

The Strangers

Standing in front of an old house where
an unremarkable schoolboy first took off
my bra and ran his hand over the band
of my underwear. He never found
the oldies station on the radio. I stuck
gum under his bed. Hot grass curled
in his cleats. Cold lemonade. The Venus
Flytrap traded from a butcher's
yard sale on the window. Nothing spelled out
from the seeds of inedible fruit smashed
on the sidewalk. He moved away
and has children now. I returned
to our hometown. I never wanted to.
Recently, a stranger confessed his GPS
speaks more kindly to him than his wife.
He then kissed me. I didn't return
a secret. I'll never see him again. Yesterday,
at the sushi bar, my dress was unzipped, the skin
of my back slick and pink from falling
asleep outside. A handsome man helped
cinch the silk together. I have no trouble eating
anything raw. The horseradish and imitation
fish went on pretending. Later, I took him
to my dirty, aging apartment. I live
alone— letting out each dove
from a ruined cathedral. *I want you
to think I'm beautiful*, I said, my eyes
half-closed. Out by the meridian
of the street, an old woman appears. *Can I
help you?* There is no shelter
in telling someone about a life
they didn't live. I get back
in my car. There are different
freckles in the afterlife.

Still, Life with Fruit

Aanjir: Figs mirror bats.   A dark knowledge —
                 hanging in lines,   feral, swinging garden
                 cradled in themselves.   Feline-faced anti-angels
                 drape from the roof.   Hugged in wings. انجیر

Anar: *Granata!* If only the pin were just the thick star of a pomegranate. انار

Gajar: Biting down a blade to coin the body. *Halwa* chewed
            on a hungry Eid with *falooda*-stained teeth. Nani says to eat more
            for healthier eyes—whose visions are these? گاجر

Kela: The word for banana in Hindi is in proximity
            to the word for loneliness. I've shared
            twinned *a-kela-ness* with many — unfolding
            the stringy veils of our richness. کیلا

Mooli: In Manhattan, carrying a bouquet of radishes. Earth buds:
            spiced white and tectonic pink. Roots waltzed with loam,
            and sunlight appeared as a ligature. Hemmed letters of glow. مولی

Nashpati: Sweet halves
                in the shapes of ears part
                to respond to dormant sweetness.

                Holding two spring bodies
                in my hands: A *pair* is not *pear*;
                the rules of three in a still life. ناشپاتی

Saape: The American alphabet starts with an apple. After *salaat*, Ma begins
            cutting fruit. Skin spirals into rosettes from desert reptiles. سیب

Your Name: Before death, you are granted paradise if you speak the Shahada.
               What if your name is my Shahada? Hawks take back the air—
               and foxes fill fevered throats with mother's milk. Ma says drink
               this in Urdu. I understand. Keep this secret. شب بخی

On Hunger

Isn't that funny? An oyster has no mind,
just a mouth. Does it feel
pleasure? My sweetheart whispers, latitudes
and oceans apart from a historic apartment
in Montmarte. The French call
oysters *fruits de mer.* What does it mean
to be broken into while living? The gravity of being opened
to break, chiseled by a stone over a stone
as if to make a sculpture. Imbued in the light
only the shipwrecked see. I, too, just want to be a mouth.
To just speak prayers of bewilderment. My masses
of nerves, no mind, tangled around this body.
What if each oyster is also a voice? Oceanic
hymn, each folded fascicle. Then, a wave
of sensuality. *I've eaten the center of a Rodin.*
I sent the beloved a letter. I was bereft
for weeks. Until their hands unfolded me
towards this nucleation. It said: *I want to be*
with you, too. I meant that I wanted to be
the other mouth in all the meals we won't share,
repeating this is an impossible
hunger wherever we are.

The Waiters

Blued rags in my hands. We eat
shooed seconds of half-gods—
under each plate, quarter moons
hide before glow. In the parking lot

after bleached tables, we gaze over
rainbows, outerglint on asphalt,

from the gas station. Holding fires
to purple mouths—a strike of a momentary beauty.

With tired hands, generous still
-to-smooth waves—we are each other's

tangled hair in nets. In the tight embrace
of no embers, no control over light.
Undoing my unlovely ponytail, caught dark

hair freed into directions of clocked-out air—
there are no borders. In your palms softening

your name over callus in Nastaliq.

Alone, in Halves

Before incineration, my father's eyeball
was placed into a plastic bag like a carnival
goldfish or lamb delved into butcher's
portions. As a child, I saw the head
of an animal my father slaughtered
displayed on ice. Once ununited,
the body is never part of it again.
Memories of how a *zamindar's* mute
child was gifted multiple tongues:
arranged and alight on a woven bed
of white silk. From each came the dark
whimper of something's last
electricity before death. A severed ear
in Lahori, dust remembers the morning
prayer played on the radio. How much
is about the displaced heart? Nothing
speaks without a body. My father's retina
frayed, devastating for a weaver—his remaining
eye without a partner. I, too, desire intimacy.
Where instead of asking —
how are you? We ask: *what did you see?*
In lieu of bouquets for new lovers,
we offer litanies of vision—betrayal
of pink cat-mouth peonies blooming
in the neighbor's garden. Shaded drips
of constellations falling from the faucet
of a wet April night—the ripped net
from an armful of burst oranges I notice
one star. I've become undone. Loss is a headless god.

Divinities

I was a winged child in Lahore,
with the sun's preening and beats
of rain, I crafted a private alphabet
from the charcoal spotted and smeared
darkness on my waterlines. Savored
gelled eggs cradled in ج, a lone father
seahorse and ate delicacies into ح.
My roti sunk into the hum of dusk.
Intoxicated in the wine-fruit of بِ
I let fall the nuqtas, like pearls, one by one,
onto the eager mouths of minnows.
|||||||| blades of grass—arched
into the fangs of an aleph. I clutched
ع onto a fleeting genesis. Everything was
in the throat of the world. Then, I
started to forget. The maenads
night-bit Orpheus into pieces,
for his lack of song. For in grieving,
the mouth is the first part
of the body to die. They threw his lips
into the maggoted-soil. There, it opened
into م م م lips on a stem. My cousin
has green eyes. A sign of our otherness
as the descendants of Alexander the Great.
Yet, I don't feel descended from a lineage
of bloodthirst. I look down
into a year. Then, another. As if I could
cup its contents into the shape
my hands make in *dua*. I saw
a dark I hadn't seen before. *Oh, Rabb.*
I want only to know you. How do I make
bird calls and know it isn't an echo?

And the Word for Moonlight is My Name

Hello.

                                           Chandini. چاندنی

This mouth is a wound
      from where I'm learning how
to love. *My love language*, I've told strangers, *is words*
         of affirmation. In naked brag
              of my American tongue—how does it taste

      to love with this Indian
         body? I knew love being breastfed
through a nightstorm after the blue song
      of electricity ended. I parse each numerical line

      about starshine that arrives in tallies. *Chandini*, I've been
         the type of Western methods
            coward who never listens

to my stomach's knowledge. I've taken
feverous temperatures with my hands.
    Then, gently slapped the trust
        of the thermometer on my knee
            and into a baby's mouth

    again. My nails are embedded with rinds of sweet oranges—
        always seeking the reach of knives.

Tell me the way
    the Bengal smells, a sweet perfume
nonexistent in a glass on my bedside table.
    Tell me again the way we could have known

    how half-gods carrying pipes with cloven hoofs
        sang in key to the slunk ring of rickshaws —
            the exhaust settled in laundry lines like blackbirds.

    How to say my own name with the certainty of a dove
trusting the buoying ark of humanity. My bird ring
    patient and sliding on the tattoo of a birdcage.

    Tell me again, Chandini.
        How divinity was without border control,
            and conversing with the sky was common as rain.

Ma used to preserve each of her calling cards in a glass
    vase as if they could blossom as if they were the umbilical
rope tethering cosmonauts to the space station.

    Given electric lines of your uncut braid,
        like an old telephone line operator,
            where can I connect it to, other than just myself?

Hello.

                Chandini. چاندنی

I've held your hair with the softness of space saints
washing each other bare
    in zero gravity. Long-distance,
        on the other side, I'll be there,

    a voyager grounded after cosmic exile.
        My breath was on the line,
            just praying against echoes.

Hello.

Chandini. چاندنی

Salam. سلا

On Borrowing Noam Chomsky

In bed, a stranger asks —
what is your relationship

to politics? To anarchy? *Organized*,
he untangles the long, black braid

of my hair, *yet, my other lovers say
my politics are a mess,* I respond.

I only know one thing:
the most beautiful word

in any language
is the name of your beloved.

Aleph From What Was Once a Homeland

Ek/ ایک

Ma Jaan holds ح from the end
of the clean-cotton of our *kurtas*,
British-English scented still

with Lahore. What is in its belly?
One pomegranate seed: ج
Three pomegranate seeds: چ

Ma places an old, gold pin in her mouth,
unmedaling her hair. Cutting the dead
-ends of braids ل in our front yard

to discard with the only working scissors
in the house. Lithe limbs of Kali
sprout another. Amphibians mimic

the goddess of death. Sieving through
my hair with yellow combs, searching
for roots that have become tinder,

others want to be on fire. Mama Jaan buries
hair into the underworld by the perennials. We go
to the *nikah* of two Pakistani strangers.

Dho / دو

At night, in the rain, over my shalwar-kameez,
a slunk, thrifted angora coat, the thickness
of my father's knuckle hair. Blooming

from the mountains of his fists. Once,
I found a stray black rabbit. Its dead
language transmitted in the swivel-scissor ears

of its fear. After an evening of hiding in
||||||||| the moonshine became mud. Then,
tracks of suburban mutts; I was once quick

to wash turmeric-gilding the underline
of my nailbeds. د became a cuticle, a little
ر rabbit's foot touched infrequently.

Theen/ تین

Kufli glisters onto the tile after colorless
sheen of another empty venue. Spilled biryani
forgotten. Here come the crows again, here

the pigeons, emerald-green of the Pakistani
flag that leans tired in my parent's garage.
The cold snout of the neighbor's dog: ه

Char/ چار

She alway greets hello. The neighbor does not.
Once, warm with bunny's blood, the grit
of her tongue. How many pomegranate kernels

are in my belly? Hymning on like Persephone
beneath the dayblaze, underworld combing her
hairline. What strata of the fossil record

are the jeweled rind and seeds mistaken
for small teeth? A lacuna, a spring
grows after loss. How lavish the garbage

before the hawk-light, before the piledriver
will pick up our gross bouquets of marigold
on a Tuesday. Again, the rabbits. رر

Madonna Arms

The dark garage
of my heart is full of gloves.
I dance there with cold palms.
In my dream, octopi cursive
and shift colors. The odorous sea
in a lover's salty palm
is a morningtide. What I want most
is to have multiple limbs. A litany
of different hearts. How much
can I hold? Fear is embedded
in all of us. It is what keeps us alive.
Night makes blue. Nightmaker yellow.
I feel afraid or anxious first
in my hands. Grooves of red nails
and charred fingertips, callus
of cratered mounds recall satellites
ringing Saturn. Each time a new
manicurist asks, *do you have*
a boyfriend? I respond
I have lovers. Between the skin,
the acetone burns my fingers.
She holds hands with a failure-
contender for a wife. I, then, am French
-manicured. Ma cried on her wedding day.
What colors does she dream into?
I want tallies for limbs. I want to be
a godstorm. One of my hands against
my ear, translating my song
twinless. The other hand holds
back the swing of night's bell. One ring
for *creator*. The second for *destroyer*.
My other arm is for her. My other
arm is for you.

One Red Thread

Caminante, a pomegranate knows itself
      as numerous. There is a world, and it is here—
           inside this one. Woven with a naked light,
my Voyager 1. *A tú manera si no con bandera.*
      Oh, and my *Caminante*,
           Voyager 1 journeyed
further than anyone, or anything, before. Did it look back
      over its shoulder, the same gaze
           of your blued departure to the borderlands?
Este retrato de Júpiter eres tú. Through hands
      and bread, we eat *Nihari* (نهار) ,
           Arabic for morning, an aubade
of the body. Turning on the flames,
      pozole was once cooked
           from human flesh. *We believe*
people are a type of maize,
      lining hominy into a vertebrate.
           I'd devour your simple hunger,
El mundo es mundo. Your lips
      are two cochineal beetles or clouds pushed
           together to create such wrinkled time.
Tooth of your red kernel is spoken for
      in these spheres. I'd take *granata* always
           over a grenade. I've held each of your hands.
Caminante, our souls bristle in a field. Combed
      with the magnetic fields of stars. Our someday
           making *roti* and *tostada*
           as round as a horse's eye or the moon.

In Dead Horse Point, We Are Alone,

and you are telling me your new father
is being deported, riding past rivers

unrushed by summer. *Look*. This is how
our world has been this fragile, how we are cut
from the navel and scattered. Desert water

evaporates before it wets *Lahori* lines
of orange trees. The fruit that taught us how to slice
our world. *Naranja* or *Naarangi* is a tart tautology.

Rhyming with nothing in America, a vibrating echo
in both Spanish and Hindi. *Naarangi*
traveled from India to Spain and was handed

in ravished fists, like the Earth itself, by Marco Polo
to hungry monarchs. Crystallized and jeweled
arancini in Sicily. Carried in sweetened braids

of a small bride, or the dead-eyed unanimal
glint of guns, as tangy *naranja*
into the New World. Silently

"j" is left out there hanging
from its hook. It was half-night. Whispering
midnight is *aadhi-raat*. We leaned again on

the silver beams of a motorcycle sweetly christened
El Burro. Circling darkened eyes, tying
hammocks from Aspen trees, sewn out and in

air eddies of hummingbirds.
Covered in pine needles, we pointed,
singing names back in English. In Spanish.

In Hindi. How can we say *Father? Walls?*
Together? Escape? Sloughed skin
of rattlesnake breaks through

and under chains. The skin bleached
white in silverhurry of moon's or *chandini's*
reflection. A spiral worn soft as the hand-

me-downs of our starving brown
grandmothers: *Abuela* and *Nani* across
latitudes who once ate orange

out of oranges, down to smiles
of slithering pulp and rind.
Rinsing my hands under the metallic tips

of common stars —
if we were to do it again, ride and die again
with you, *El Burro*, out there at half-night,

this time, ride and die again,
in the warm breath of our tent, I'd say
Salam and hold you so

with the American choreography
of a pigskin flying
to be caught

by a child, whose real father,
like yours, rode and died
and only returned

once.

How to Make an Ariel

For Nani Jaan

I've taken your shoes. Our feet
    are the same size, nothing else. Naked
foot where I touch an estuary

    of tubule-tender lines. Rambling into
a tarpan, heart beating with the warm rave
    of being a winning racehorse. Legs in a gait,

    I'm an unfaithful alphabet. Unwrung
English papers in the laundry room are slack
    warm sails that smell of the sea. The wet

humidity of my foreign palms. I am the hoof
    of us, recording every pain of every stone
that trots on the nail. The way we canter on it.

How muted my tantrum when you pointed
    to the unclean gravestone of my other grandmother.
Unknowable hypsometry of raised and curved

letters that I ran my blind hands repeatedly.
    What does it say? A rolling wave of unknowing.
Do you love me, master? All my dreams are in English.

    Back at my Ma's childhood home,
I banded light. The generator deafening.
    Reading Shakespeare and practicing Urdu

in the bathtub, you call me *Chandini*, moonlight. چاندنی
    Only so long before a lost American
mermaid can stand without floating on into foam.

Where are we from sea level? How close to the lost
psalm written by walks intertwined —arm and fin.
　　　The rhythm made by feet clopping in

your bathroom slippers? In the wilds of myself,
　　　I *consider* you everywhere. In lines
of Paiute sandstone and burning sagebrush, I know

considerare shares an etymological root with *sidus*, or star.
　　　You have held me in the gaze of the most patient eye.

Painting shadows at the pace of a lunar mare.

Con la Serpiente

Tu boca manchada de granada. How many seeds
did you eat this winter? Dragging fur of burrs
from The Underworld into these cold-human
            New York streets and parks. How many dogs
              did you see with three heads? To evade the laughter
            of a stranger's eyes. Abril, *Lejana y sola.*

Conoceme esta noche según tus manos. I'm your nailbeds
filled with flakes of my life before sleep. In April,
an electric unplugged eel in wet parenthesis.
            Speaking in octaves, searching for variations
            of hunger to speak to myself
            about your pomegranate-stained lips.

Mi lengua es esta serpiente   Mi lengua es esta serpiente   Mi lengua es esta serpiente

      In Utah, on our knees, we witness
      serpents in wildflowers, mushroom circles
      like shoaling whales pooling around schools of fish.
Abril, *Lejana y sola.*
            Te seguiría a un inframundo

All things are cyclic. The swivel of an animal
that hears danger, Earth keeps returning
to the same position as our birthdays.
                      I am in Harlem, again —
                      someone has taken your mattress
                      from the curb. You circumnavigate
the way blood journeys
through my body, too. Moving on
in cyclic migration,
                      or is it an instinctual movement?

Towards Tenderness, A Knife

Nani couldn't keep on living
without knowing the great voice of death.
   In her hands,
her last bird, cooing—*Ajo*. آو آو آو آو
   Come on, in Urdu. The body
    rises for a moment. A boat bouncing
on trembles of waves. Spreading her hands
like a blind ascetic
   gathering paradise.
Circumnavigating fingers
on fat, ligneous neck, grazing—
   a fishing line
along the water, latitudes of home.
Comforting the chicken
   with palms that envelope mine.
Folding together
the dough, secret as fascicles
   to hide in drawers under saris, white
wiped vermillion. The false breast
I once discovered, mistaking it
   for actual flesh
that Nani rushed to hide again.
Hear the whip
   of her three-pronged braid, swaying—
grown after chemo, a war medallion.
Breaching the neck
   with her favorite knife.
Calm as separating
meat from the pit of a peach.
   She hands me the heart.
A Ma who grew my Ma inside—
an immigrant to both worlds,
   could end a life, just as tender.
Later, I ask my Nani to send me her hair

from overseas. A gilt thread to weave
    on the throat
of my wrist, the same
length as my own,
    to dare the stained shadow of death—*Ajo.* آو آو آو

The Flood

1. Ark

We eat clementine halves on bedsheets. Circled like sun
in love's redeeming stains. A thirst that rolls each wave.
Lives spent devoted to comprehending an appetite.

On a cornflower-colored mattress, the world floats
on the fins of blue sharks. There, pulp and floods of nirvana
of teeth and teeth. We are far and obscure in hidden water.

2. Dove

Love nothing as brief as clouds. Only the sun makes love
as hot as the salt off the mule's rocky shoulders,
the mane braided with dandelions, each labor gently

bribed with sugarcubes to bite the bit. I dare you:
gift me your faith. Once, fingers tattooed with birdcages.
We are rings of doves. I know this glide is like a bow.

In the Throats of Wild Things

A Catholic saint blesses the unwing
of the throat and all wild animals. The brute

tongue that resides in both, I've caught
in myself a wildness. The injured

frog cried part eye, part skin
in its recognition. Asking to be healed,

I, too, am amphibian song, the dark field.
The regeneration of the heart in all

of its impossible unfoldings
without an ambit. My mind lives in these

twin skins returned: how slow
this wheel is. The kinetic fluid nest

of salamander eggs floating on a lone
cloud above the mountain, I cupped

in the shape of prayer. A body
of water, once polluted. Reverted back

with the unruly sky into clarity
through mycological regeneration.

How will you heal me?

asks the widow, the spider ashed
in a shooed corner, the nirvana

of teeth among other teeth. The unloved
hounds at the ankles of the saint after

trapped and poisoned. Let me pretend
I believe in something. A miracle:

the discovery of a species of birds
that makes garlands out of thorns.

It is not enough for me to become
a believer. What will be enough?

The belly-up fish turned back
to abandoned bluegrass femur-long.

Of salamanders jellied in a pond.
How Kali is an ecologist,

and saints are not the way I know
creation and destruction. The limb

made into a mother of thousands.
No matter what prayer you answer.

Here are the cycles of remaking —
my patch of red and sour feral

strawberries, each a different
size of my finger.

Haptics of Blue

The smallness of language between
us, the day before Krishna Janmashtami,

we line up outside the temple. The guru
marks red our foreheads. Lost in ventricles

of divine unconcern. In tender protest,
my world is another color. Lorca: *Verde que*

te quiero verde. Some lovemaking becomes
silent labor, windless and starless midnights.

Yesterday's lapse of repeated myths.
What I don't know is how to love

another person. How will I remember
your wet, tangled hair smelled of kelp?

An exit sign exhales. I tell you, *so, I want*
to come clean. In the parking lot, our private

ceremonies—a water bottle, your gentle face—
I am now pouring into each hand.

Con La Serpiente Pt. II

Sleeping in craggy eights, deforming
socks and bedsheets. The fever
of the heatlamp watches the cat-eye
yellow of its prowl. Every escape
is an art form. God created
the serpent from mercury,
the glassy mirror in the basement.
To not frighten the mindless
and tender creatures lopping
in the field. The night opens
a faucet of metallic light, the usual
chores. There, an ambush of stars
in a new dark. Now, each peel
of our skin in the kitchen
slinks on like gnarled bouquets
over a burial place. Between us—
sometimes that genre of silence.
We wash and eat bruised
strawberries swallowed whole.
Pink as tongues. Small as eyes.
It frightens me how much we can love
when starving. Where is the cage
now? Make of us
little beasts.

Pegasus Tattoo on the Left

A horse is a muscular hyphen—
connecting humans to nighttides of the open
      animal world beyond us. Last night I dreamt
      that you married someone who wasn't me.
A winged horse is a regatta of stars—
human's first spacecraft, the moon, too,
      is a changing hoof. How far upwards
      each verve of the earth, a lunarship searching
for unknown fruit. The tail, a brush of a comet's
glitterfreeze. I've sailed on these half-wings.
      The dream rivets to silent, deep space.
      The event horizon: an open gate.
The cold ocean is not a horse —
Mare and *mer*: false cognates.
      Lunar mare: dark waves
      of basalt, ancient stargazers misunderstood
to be water, *maria*. Pronounce this, *Medusa*.
Sidus signs of your tongue on the lateral
      of my dark thighs. An odious oasis, a desert
      mer. Snakeskin glints in impastos of sage:
layers of landscape. I'll take handfuls
home with your old jackknife. I'll siren into
      chalk-smoke motes, shadowed patterns
      on celestial bodies. The mane falls wild
on my black coat. White heat from the planets
cantered light from behind the plateau.
      How far of a dive into *la mer* until each creature
      becomes eyeless?   Come, now out of the sing of river —
drink a godsong like horses out of green
buds about to speak into spring.

Brief Conversation with a Little Moon

Even this planet bears secrets, Little Moon.
Little Moon, you are an unfaithful lover roped in
    without siphoning the morning sky for clues.

A lover's hair that accidentally spells out love in cursive
    pulled into orbit with our vision concomitant
on both your glittering leaving and faint arrival.

There is no such thing as shared time in space,
    just private choreographies. We are often late
to the dance: two years of you, چاندنی and no light

    of knowledge, just cosmic squatting in an unseen circuit
above us without discovery. Gravity, a quiet thief pockets
    small, cold unforever coins of the Universe.

Claims bodies with a bright sickle
    of wonder. Reaping in glitterfreeze,
sintering a handful of orbits, and then releasing.
    What will you tell the rest, Little Moon?

About what you witnessed on Earth?
    When will you return? Could we be just be
another dim stone on the cairn of your travels?

    Little Moon, scuttled between planets
you are a silvered minnow, invisible to the naked eye that opens
    her mouth in warm zeroes. Then you will go

back into the dark ravine of an infinity

    that goes on without our favors, without our desires.

The Passenger

Neon gnawing dusk, a stranger I was riding
with pulled up to a gas station, cigarettes and venison
jerky, the plastic reflecting long teeth of city lights
and conifer air fresheners. Earlier, I had pointed
out the window. *Deer!* Then came the dead;
a body alchemized into a grotesque
shape: the swan neck broken, eyes dark
with a savage kindness. There, from living
to carcass. Metaphor's raw flesh is shaped
into something unlike any animal. Always, I am
startled by beauty's lawlessness. The stranger
bites into the jerky; *Here*, he says, *you must be
so hungry*. In undergrad, a wealthy girl, perfect blood-
red nails wrote of her hunter father,
an alcoholic. In grad school, a small-town girl,
Moby Dick memorized, penned a poem
about deep poverty, her father bringing home
roadkill, an albino deer. The family ate without
remorse that it was exceptional. What have I seen
through varied windows? Inside the station,
local art trinkets carved from wood, a moose,
a two-headed calf, and nameplates never bearing
my name. A sculpture catches my eye,
more a scale, a suspended rotation of coal,
and a lightbulb tethered by driftwood,
coal's weightiness obvious. Then, a portrait
of the artist: a dead coal miner with a black lung. Imagine
his hands. His tender bread. The contours of his
young wife. I understand. After arriving at the motel,
I leave the lights off. The stranger went away
to his room. I sleep on a worn sheet
of perfect darkness and drape it over
the next deer.

The Neighbors

Narcoleptic porch light swings envious,
moths are nebulous sculptors of the bluedark.

Light. Night. Hollowing circles, shaping bedfellows
in rhyme. The collie sleepwhimpers at my feet. Tremors

of stars find partners and perform a semaphore.
A bright, common moon emerges, baying for canines

from between pines— desperate for devotion.
Arriving like a dead star's flash, I see eyes

in the next-door driveway. There she is, my neighbor,
exhaling profanities for a lover. She always leaves

her lights on, and the lawn grows femur-high. She notices
me, ashes the orange dot of her cigarette and waves

hello —as if I am an old friend. I mouth
a muted *salam*. سلام. Hello, stranger.

We have never spoken. It doesn't matter
if I make myself dinner now or keep on waving—

I'll still wake up hungry.

Notes

"The Stringing of the Bow" refers to "arrowy one, when you whir toward me/ I know from where/ I forget from where from" by Paul Celan, from "A Ring, for Bowdrawing," tr. by Pierre Joris. Second, this poem was born as a tribute and ode to a poem I often repeat before sleep, "Two Headed Calf," by Lauren Gilpin.

"Marrow of Mercy" references the "Eyes of a Blue Dog" (1950) by the master, Gabriel García Márquez. I first read this short story on a bus ride from Salt Lake City to Portland. Since then, I have thought of it almost daily. In addition, I first sketched this poem in the margins of Judas Goat (Tin House, 2023) by Gabrielle Bates. So thankful to both of these G's.

"The Strangers" is not an autobiographical poem. Yet, I wrote this poem on a napkin eating sushi.

"Still Life with Fruit" is dedicated to Harryette Mullen.

"On Oysters" was written after Natalia visited Can Cisa-Bar Brutal in Barcelona, where she learned this piece of zoological trivia, which ignited this poem. We went to Can Cisa-Bar Brutal just before my chapbook was published. I thought about taking one of the glossy oyster shells as a memento, but my purse was too small, and everyone would have noticed if I tried to slip it into my shirt.

"The Waiters" would not have been possible without my friend, the poet and painter, Basie Allen waking up early one Brooklyn morning and whittling this little ode to yearning and restaurant life into what it needed to be. In addition, Nastaliq refers to the calligraphic script most widely now associated with Persian, Urdu, and other South Asian languages. Further, the script is evoked by the stylized non-Roman letters in this chapbook.

The term "zamindar" in "Alone, In Halves" refers to a feudal ruler of an estate. This poem specifically denotes the landowners who, in collaboration with the British Raj, collected taxes from farmers. Further, this poem is for my father who lost vision in one of his eyes during the ongoing pandemic.

"One Red Thread" evokes the Devendra Banhart song "Samba Vexillographica" with the phrase, "A tú manera si no con bandera." Many thanks to Devendra Banhart for being my favorite artist to listen to in the mornings when I can't walk between the ecotone of sleep and waking life.

"In Dead Horse Point, We are Alone," Dead Horse Point State Park overlooks the Colorado River and Canyonlands National Park. It also featured in the iconic final scene of the 1991 film *Thelma & Louise*. The etymology knowledge was taken from an article in *Bon Appetit* titled "The Etymology of the Orange" by Sam Dean, which was published in February 2013.

"How to Make an Ariel" evokes the trinity of Ariels: *The Tempest, The Little Mermaid,* and Sylvia Plath.

In the Catholic tradition, St. Blaise is best known for his miraculous healings, particularly of animals and people suffering from throat ailments. "In the Throats of Wild Things" also references Kali, a significant and complex Hindu deity revered as the goddess of time, change, power, creation, preservation, and destruction.

"Haptics of Blue" references the first lines of "Romance sonámbulo"/ "Sleepwalking Romance" by Federico García Lorca. Thank you. For showing us the way. In addition, Krishna Janmashtami, also known as Janmashtami or Gokulashtami, is a Hindu festival that celebrates the birth of Lord Krishna, the eighth avatar of Vishnu.

Last, a larger note for this series of poems is that I am someone who is neither from here nor there. Great care and consideration were placed on honoring all theological, cosmological, and linguistic traditions present and evoked in these poems. If I have made any errors, please forgive me, reader. Thank you.

Acknowledgements

First, thank you, reader.

To my family, my beloveds, and the vast, unknowable mystery surrounding us.

Thank you for the moments of daydreaming at the table. To my Nani Jaan, Rani Tahzeen Mirza, and my Papa, who took me on late-night rides into the dark blue and filled our home with lyricism. My gratitude extends to Mama Jaan for the daily roti and salaan created by your hands. Thanks, Mom. I owe you everything.

My heartfelt thanks to my editor, Adrie Rose, and the students of Smith College. Your insightful feedback and contributions, including the cover design, have been invaluable.

I am grateful to my mentors who first believed in my potential as a poet: Aracelis Girmay, Major Jackson, Jay Depshande, Cynthia Cruz, Timothy Donnelly, Deborah Paradez, Alan Gilbert, Shane McCrae, Monica Youn, Katharine Coles, Paisley Rekdal, Stephen Goldsmith, Brett Clark, especially Dr. Brett Clark.

A warm thank you to my peers at Columbia University: Mark Gregory Lopez, Shayanne Figueroa Bennett, Elias Sorich, Timothy Emile Lax, Antonio Addessi, Emma Ginader, Peter Patapis, Robiny Jamerson, and Rachel Kang. Your time, notes, and patience have been deeply appreciated, and thank you for not getting upset with my daily crunching on apples and messy peanut butter in class.

Gratitude from my bones to my friends, co-artists, and muses: Cameron J. Jorgensen, Dane J. Horton, Patrick J.Bayly, Basie Allen, Aaron H. Aceves, Jack Scott Holmes, Nat Blanton, Grayson del Faro, David Lenz, Gianpierre Sato, Caleb Milne, Jeff Sorensen, Jonah King, Corley Miller, Daniel Leipow, Jordan Nemelka, Zakary Sonntag, Amber Aumiller, Rylee Syme, Erica O'Brien, Blaise Swing, and Maxwell Ijams.

Finally, to Natalia C. Abril, especially Natalia. The world is the world, and you helped me shape this one.

My deepest thanks and prayers to the following writers: Mei-Mei Berssenbrugge, W.G. Sebald, Anna Akhmatova, Jorie Graham, Paul Celan, Marina Tsvetaeva, Cecilia Vicuna, Anne Carson, Louise Glück, Charles Wright, James Wright, Frank Stanford, Lucie Brock-Borido, Jim Harrison, W.S. Merwin, Linda Gregg, and Brigit Pegeen Kelly.

Thank you to everyone at Publik in The Avenues, City, Mazza on 15th and 15th, The Rose Establishment in Downtown SLC, Devocion in Brooklyn, Tazo in Washington Heights, Community Food and Juice, and The Hungarian Pastry Shop in Morningside Heights. These places have been more than mere physical spaces; thank you. Centennial Valley, Montana, and Morningside Heights, New York—two places that have felt like home.

Lastly, this life and these words would not be possible without my beloved partner, Dr. John Christopher Dulin. I love you beyond all of this.

Thank you to the following journals, where some of these poems first appeared.

Stringing the Bow, *The Virginia Quarterly*

Marrow of Mercy, *Australian Poetry Jounral*

Still, Life with Fruit, *Brushfire Magazine*

The Waiters, *The American Poetry Review*

Aleph From What Was Once a Homeland, *The Denver Quarterly*

On Hunger, *The Southern Humanities Review*

In Dead Horse Point, We Are Alone, *The American Poetry Review*

One Red Thread, *Borderlands: Texas Poetry Review*

How to Make an Ariel, *The Margins, Asian American Writer's Workshop*

Towards Tenderness, A Knife, *SLUG Magazine*

And the Word for Moonlight is My Name, *POETRY Magazine*

Pegasus Tattoo on the Left, *Four Way Review*

Brief Conversation with a Little Moon, *Ligea Magazine*

In the Throats of Wild Things, *Image Journal*

The Flood, *The Raleigh Review*

Haptics of Blue, *Image Journal*

Con La Serpiente Pt. II, *Small Orange Journal*

The Strangers, *The Amsterdam Review*

The Passenger, *The Oxonian Review*

The Neighbors, *The Arkansas International*

Jai Hamid Bashir is a South Asian artist whose work has been featured in publications such as *POETRY, American Poetry Review, The Rumpus, The Arkansas International, Black Warrior Review, Denver Quarterly*, and *Image Journal*. A graduate of the University of Utah and Columbia University, she lives and writes in the American West with her partner.

This book was designed by Margaret W. Valle in spring 2024 at Smith College. It was set in Times New Roman and Bodoni 72. Times New Roman is a serif typeface designed by Stanley Morison Victor Lardent and released in 1932. Bodoni 72 is a serif typeface designed by Giambattista Bodoni.